YOUR KNOWLEDGE HAS VALUE

AF150210

- We will publish your bachelor's and master's thesis, essays and papers

- Your own eBook and book - sold worldwide in all relevant shops

- Earn money with each sale

Upload your text at www.GRIN.com and publish for free

Sabrina Travis

Form and Meaning of Wordsworth's "Composed upon Westminster Bridge, September 3, 1802"

GRIN Verlag

Bibliografische Information der Deutschen Nationalbibliothek:

Die Deutsche Bibliothek verzeichnet diese Publikation in der Deutschen National-
bibliografie; detaillierte bibliografische Daten sind im Internet über http://dnb.d-
nb.de/ abrufbar.

Imprint:

Copyright © 2012 GRIN Verlag GmbH
Druck und Bindung: Books on Demand GmbH, Norderstedt Germany
ISBN: 978-3-656-49252-8

This book at GRIN:

http://www.grin.com/en/e-book/232237/form-and-meaning-of-wordsworth-s-com-
posed-upon-westminster-bridge-september

Universität Trier

Fachbereich II/ Anglistik

LING 401/meth – Linguistic Stylistics (of Literary Texts) (SoSe 2012)

Form & Meaning of Wordsworth's "Composed upon Westminster Bridge, September 3, 1802"

Sabrina Ackermann

English Language, Linguistic and Literature/ Deutsch als Fremdsprache

Submission: August 23rd, 2012

Table of Contents

1. Introduction _____ 3

2. Linguistic Features _____ 3

    2.1 The Vocabulary _____ 4

        2.1.1 The Use of Negatives _____ 4

        2.1.2 Lexical Fields _____ 4

    2.2 The Discourse Sequence _____ 6

    2.3 Cultural Reference _____ 6

3. The Role of The Reader and Their Expectations _____ 7

    3.1 The Knowledge of London _____ 7

    3.2 The Knowledge of The Author and The Literary Genre _____ 8

4. Conclusion _____ 9

5. References _____ 10

6. Appendix _____ 11

    1) Wordsworth: "Composed upon Westminster Bridge, September 3, 1802"

    2) Wordsworth: "The World Is Too Much With Us"

    3) Wordsworth: "I Wandered Lonely as a Cloud"

1. Introduction

"Earth has not anything to show more fair" (Appendix 1, line 1). This line is the first of William Wordsworth's sonnet "Composed upon Westminster Bridge, September 3, 1802". As a romantic poet, Wordsworth usually praises nature and its beauty but this sonnet differs from his other poems. In this text, Wordsworth expresses strong feelings and emotions towards London in the 19th century. He describes London in the morning and surprisingly he is amazed by the beauty of the city itself. How far in detail this poem contrasts with other pieces by Wordsworth will be clarified in the main part.

In order to understand the poem and its meaning, it is helpful to take a closer look at different levels of description. Therefore, the aim of this paper is to provide an analysis of the main linguistic features such as the vocabulary used by Wordsworth and also the discourse structure. Additionally, it is important to consider the significance of the context, the role of the reader as well as their expectations.

2. Linguistic Features

Before looking at specific linguistic features in the sonnet, it is necessary to give a proper definition of *stylistics* and also an overview of the most important linguistic features. Peter Barry defines it as the following: "Stylistics is a critical approach which uses the methods and findings of the science of linguistics in the analysis of literary texts. (…) and its aim is to show how the technical linguistic features of a literary work, such as the grammatical structure of its sentences, contribute to its overall meanings and effects" (2009:196). So, *stylistics* basically means analyzing different levels of grammar in text with the purpose of giving "textual evidence for a particular interpretation" (Verdonk 2002:31)

But what are linguistic features? The "systematic ways of describing language use [are]: phonology, lexis, syntax, discourse sequence, [and] semantic organization" (Stubbs 2012). However, this paper focuses on the vocabulary used in the sonnet, the discourse sequence and the cultural reference.

2.1 The Vocabulary

2.1.1 The Use of Negatives

By analyzing the specific language used in the sonnet we can observe that Wordsworth made use of numerous negatives. Here, not only explicitly expressed negatives such as "not anything", in line 1, or "never", in line 9 and twice in line 11, are taken into account, also words that express the absence of something. To make this less abstract, the following examples are selected from Wordsworth sonnet. The first example is in line 8: "All bright and glittering in the smokeless air". In this instance, the absence of smoke is mentioned. But besides the explicit expression of the absence of something, we also find implicit expression. In line 5, the beauty of the morning is described as "silent" and "bare". Wordsworth portrays the morning as not covered (with dirt, fog?) and without the presence of noise. This also applies for the example in line 11: "Ne'er saw I, never felt, a calm so deep!" The city does not move, it is quiet and perhaps even peaceful. In line 13 when Wordsworth writes that "[…] the very houses seem asleep" the state of sleeping is mentioned. Or what is more decisive: the city is not (yet) awake. This pattern is then finally concluded in the last line when Wordsworth states that "all that mighty heart is lying still".

All of the examples pointed out refer to negatives or the absence of something. Moreover, a particular way of presenting London is expressed: London in the morning, described by Wordsworth, is quiet, uncovered and peaceful.

Furthermore, it is possible that the illustrated examples are perceived negative because they are in contrast to what we, as the reader, expect London to be. The capital of the United Kingdom has been a global city where the presence of noise and movements everywhere should not be unexpected. Nevertheless, Wordsworth refers to London as "silent", "calm" and "still". However, the aspect of expectations will be further discussed in 3.

2.1.2 Lexical Fields

Another way of looking at the vocabulary is to categorize words into lexical fields. In Wordsworth's sonnet "Composed upon Westminster Bridge, September 3, 1802", many different categories are to be found. The first category *nature* can already be found in the first line of the sonnet. More precisely, the first word of the sonnet is "earth". The next word is in line 7 when Wordsworth talks about "the field" and "the sky". Continuing with the next 3 lines, the words "air", "sun", "valley", "rock" and "hill" can be found. Consequently, nature has certain significance in the sonnet.

In correspondence to most of the words representing *nature* there is another lexical field that describes the beauty of nature. For example, "all bright and glittering" (l.8) refers to the field and the sky. Similarly, in line 10 "valley, rock, or hill" is described as "in his first splendour".

The next lexical field was already touched upon in 2.1.1. Here, the lexical field represents silence. Words such as "silent" (l.5), "calm" (l.11), "asleep" (l.13) and last but not least "still" (l.14) are used to describe the morning in London.

The last lexical field I would like to focus on is *city*. That means every word that represents London, the city and the buildings. The first instance occurs in the title of the sonnet. "Composed upon Westminster Bridge (…)" refers to one of London's places of interest, the Westminster Bridge. In line 4, Wordsworth explicitly mentions the city that wears the beauty of the morning (cf. l.4&5). In the development of the sonnet, further vocabulary is used to refer to the city itself. Line 6 almost completely names parts of the city such as ships, towers, domes or theaters. And the final mention is made in the 13th line where Wordsworth describes "the very houses [to] seem asleep".

Even though there are more lexical fields represented in the sonnet, I only focused on the previous ones. All of them considered, we can say that nature, the positive description of parts of it, and the city itself are the main topic of the sonnet. The nature is described as beautiful whereas the city is calm.

In the following paragraph, I will try to discuss if or if not nature and the city stand in contrast to each other by looking closer at the discourse sequence.

2.2 The Discourse Sequence

The poem is an Italian sonnet with the rhyme scheme of abbaabba cdcdcd. This shows that the sonnet can be divided into eight + six lines. The change of the rhyme scheme in line 9 introduces a change in content. Looking closer we can say that the main focus in the first eight lines is on the city. In line 4, Wordsworth talks about the city in general. In line 6, he presents man-made buildings such as "ships" or "temples". Additionally, the first eight lines are written in present tense.

Then in line 9, the focus changes and so does the tense. "Never did sun more beautifully steep". As we can see, the tense changes from present to past tense. Lines nine to twelve describe the nature in London. In the last two lines we see another change in the tense: "(...) houses seem asleep" (l.13) and "that mighty heart is lying still" (l.14). Here, the tense changes back to present tense.

But how can we understand what just has been analyzed? First of all, there is a contrast between the city and the nature. The fact that the tense changes when the focus on the city changes to the nature, makes the contrast evident. The present tense in the first eight lines could illustrate the significance of the city in the here and now. But then from line nine to line twelve the tense is past which could mean that even though the city is amazing, nature came first. The city can only be so beautiful when there is nature as well.

The last two lines bring the reader back to here and now and make clear that everybody is still "asleep" (l.13) and that the "mighty heart is lying still" (l.14). The mighty heart could then refer to the heart of the city. This aspect leads to the next theme: the cultural reference.

2.3 Cultural Reference

The title of the sonnet immediately refers to London as with the mentioning of the Westminster Bridge. It is one of London's most popular places. The Westminster Bridge connects the north side with the south of London and is placed near the Houses of Parliament.

Moreover, the additional information that the sonnet was composed in 1802 creates another cultural reference. The Industrial Revolution "began in England sometime after the middle of the 18th century" (Kreis 2011). Therefore, the revolution had a great impact on London and its people at the time the sonnet was composed. Wordsworth refers to the "ships", "towers" and "theatres" (l.6) that are parts of London. Within the Industrial Revolution, London became more powerful. It has been a global city for hundreds of years and has great influence on other countries. In his last two lines, Wordsworth might refer to the development and globalization in London. "(…) the very houses seem asleep, and all that mighty heart is lying still". He describes London in the morning with all its beauty but it becomes clear that people are not yet awake, the business and the traffic have not started yet. So, "that mighty heart" of London "is lying still" and one can enjoy the beauty of the city.

3. The Role of The Reader and Their Expectations

In order to be able to understand the meaning of the sonnet or its purpose we not only focus on the linguistic features we can find in the text but we also have to consider the knowledge of the reader. It is important to take into account that the reader knows about London and about the author as well as the literary genre of the poem. Not to forget is the knowledge of other poems by Wordsworth.

Considering all these factors, it can be assumed that the reader has expectations with regard to the text and these expectations can influence the interpretation as well as the author playing with these expectations.

3.1 The Knowledge of London

As already described in 2.3, London is a global city and was affected by the Industrial Revolution. Therefore, the reader expects London to be noisy, smoky and hectic. So as soon as the reader reads the title of the sonnet, he knows that it will be about London and therefore he associates London with the formerly mentioned adjectives. Wordsworth, however, describes London as the opposite. By using negatives he describes how he experienced London. Furthermore, using negatives shows the reader that London does not have to be as they expect.

3.2 The Knowledge of The Author and The Literary Genre

Another important aspect that influences the interpretation of the sonnet is the knowledge of the author and the genre. Wordsworth lived from 1770 to 1850 and was "one of the most popular of all English poets who started the Romantic Movement in English poetry" (Crowther 1999:589). As a Romanticist he writes "mainly about the beauty of nature and its relationship with all human beings" (Crowther 1999:589). Knowing that Wordsworth is a Romanticist allows the reader to expect him to write about a certain content or intention.

Additionally, if the reader knows other poems by Wordsworth, he will expect the sonnet to be similar to the other ones. This is called "intertextuality" and Verdonk explains it as "an allusion to another text and, at the same time, an appeal to the reader's awareness of that text" (Verdonk 2002:5). In this case we may possibly talk about "inter-textuality" because it is the systematic reference which is important. That means if the reader has read for instance "The World Is Too Much With Us", he is influenced by this sonnet. The reader is familiar with Wordsworth and his themes (Appendix 2). In this one, Wordsworth criticizes the outcome of the Industrial Revolution and that people distance themselves from nature. For him, nature plays a significant role and this is represented in most if not all sonnets he wrote.

Another example is the poem "I Wandered Lonely as a Cloud" (Appendix 3). He writes about "dancing daffodils" (l.4), the lake and trees (cf. l.5). The central theme in this sonnet is nature. For this reason, the reader expects Wordsworth to write about nature and its beauty.

Despite the fact that Wordsworth usually only praises nature, he combines his love for nature with his amazement for the beauty of London. As a romantic poet he is expected to see the beauty of nature and to portray "silence" in nature but in the sonnet "Composed upon Westminster Bridge, September 3, 1802" he portrays London as silent and calm. This aspect would then be against the expectations of the reader.

In summary, the role of the reader is significant for the interpretation of the text. Depending on the reader's knowledge and expectations the interpretation can vary and lead in different directions.

4. Conclusion

All in all, in this sonnet, linguistic features such as the vocabulary, the discourse and the context help to interpret the text. Wordsworth describes the beauty of London in the morning. His use of the vocabulary shows that he experienced the city against what people might think of London. Additionally, looking at the lexical fields and the structure of the sonnet, he shows a contrast between the city and the nature. And even though this sonnet differs from other poems by Wordsworth, it still includes aspects such as the description of beauty or his relationship to nature.

Nevertheless, and this is one of the problems stylistics has to deal with, we as the reader can only assume what Wordsworth's intentions were. For example, the use of negatives can just be a coincidence which means that he did not intend to describe London against the expectations of the reader.

Furthermore, we need to keep in mind that "we all have different expectations and different emotions, (...) and thereby our interpretation of the text (...) differs from reader to reader" (Verdonk 2002:14). So after all, it will never be possible to have the most proper interpretation.

But altogether, analyzing the form of a literary text and finding textual evidence helps to understand the meaning of it.

5. References

Barry, Peter (2009) *Beginning Theory – An Introduction to Literary and Cultural Theory*. Manchester: Manchester University Press.

Crowther, J ed (1999) *Oxford Guide to British and American Culture*. Oxford: OUP.

Kreis, Steven (2011) The Origins of the Industrial Revolution in England. *The History Guide*. http:// http://www.historyguide.org/intellect/lecture17a.html. 19 August 2012.

Stubbs, M (2012) *How to Write your Term Papers*

Verdonk, Peter (2002) *Stylistics*. Oxford: OUP.

Wordsworth, W. *Poetry Archive*. http://www.poetry-archive.com/w/wordsworth_william.html. 22 August 2012.

6. Appendix

1) UPON WESTMINSTER BRIDGE

William Wordsworth (1770-1850)

EARTH has not anything to show more fair:
Dull would he be of soul who could pass by
A sight so touching in its majesty:
This City now doth like a garment wear
The beauty of the morning; silent, bare,
Ships, towers, domes, theatres, and temples lie
Open unto the fields, and to the sky;
All bright and glittering in the smokeless air.
Never did sun more beautifully steep
In his first splendour valley, rock, or hill;
Ne'er saw I, never felt, a calm so deep!
The river glideth at his own sweet will:
Dear God! the very houses seem asleep;
And all that mighty heart is lying still!

2) THE WORLD IS TOO MUCH WITH US

William Wordsworth (1770-1850)

THE world is too much with us: late and soon,
Getting and spending, we lay waste our powers:
Little we see in Nature that is ours;
We have given our hearts away, a sordid boon!
This Sea that bares her bosom to the moon;
The winds that will be howling at all hours,
And are up-gathered now like sleeping flowers;
For this, for everything, we are out of tune;
It moves us not. -- Great God! I'd rather be
A Pagan suckled in a creed outworn;
So might I, standing on this pleasant lea,
Have glimpses that would make me less forlorn;
Have sight of Proteus rising from the sea;
Or hear old Triton blow his wreathèd horn.

3) THE DAFFODILS; OR, I WANDERED LONELY AS A CLOUD

William Wordsworth (1770-1850)

I WANDERED lonely as a cloud
That floats on high o'er vales and hills,
When all at once I saw a crowd,
A host, of golden daffodils;
Beside the lake, beneath the trees,
Fluttering and dancing in the breeze.

Continuous as the stars that shine
And twinkle on the milky way,
They stretched in never-ending line
Along the margin of the bay:
Ten thousand saw I at a glance,
Tossing their heads in sprightly dance.

The waves beside them danced; but they
Out-did the sparkling waves in glee
A poet could not but be gay,
In such a jocund company
I gazed -- and gazed -- but little thought
What wealth the show to me had brought:

For oft, when on my couch I lie
In vacant or in pensive mood,
They flash upon that inward eye
Which is the bliss of solitude;
And then my heart with pleasure fills,
And dances with the daffodils.